Animals

Coloring Pages for Relaxation and Stress Relief

© 2021

Helena Martinson

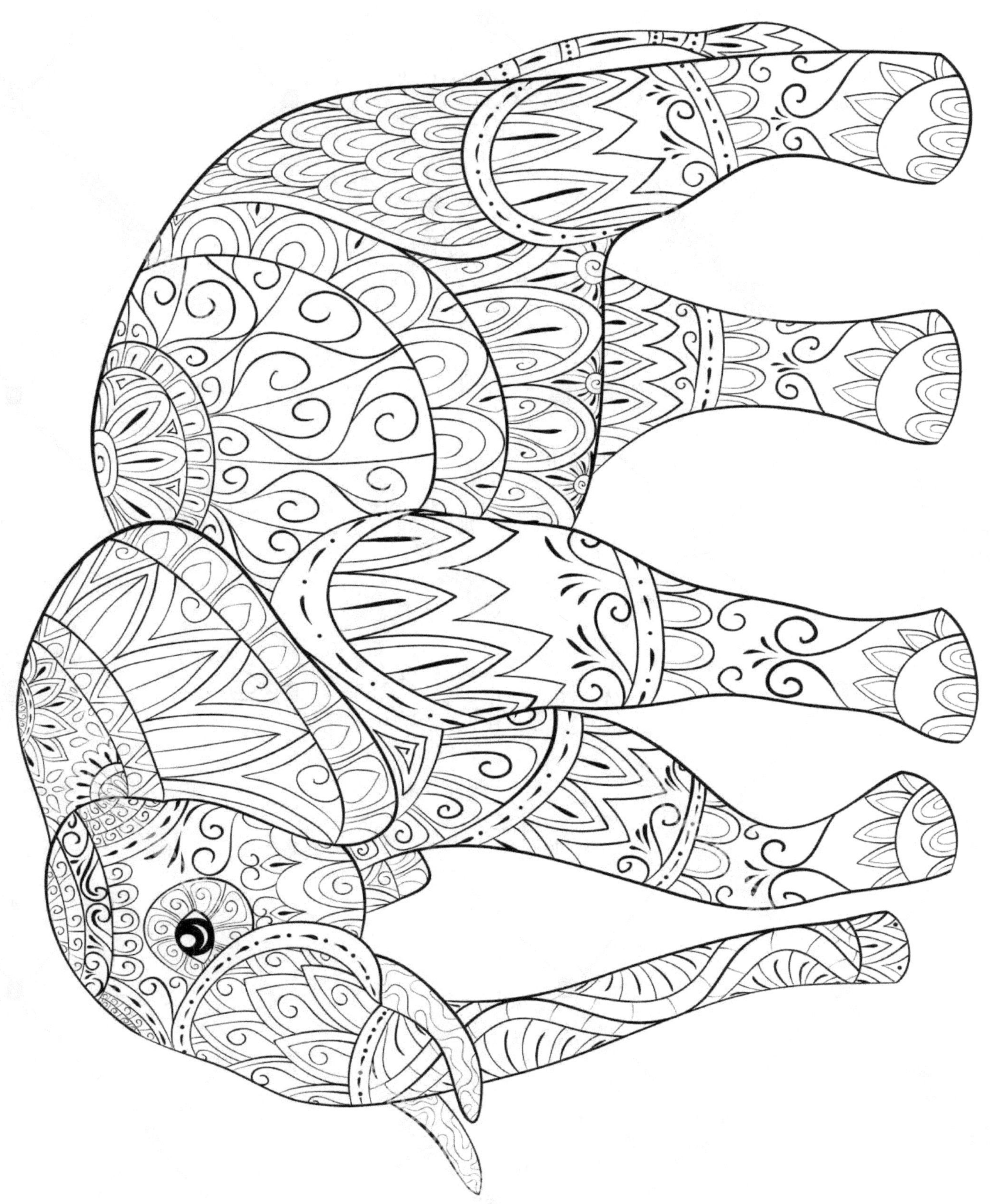

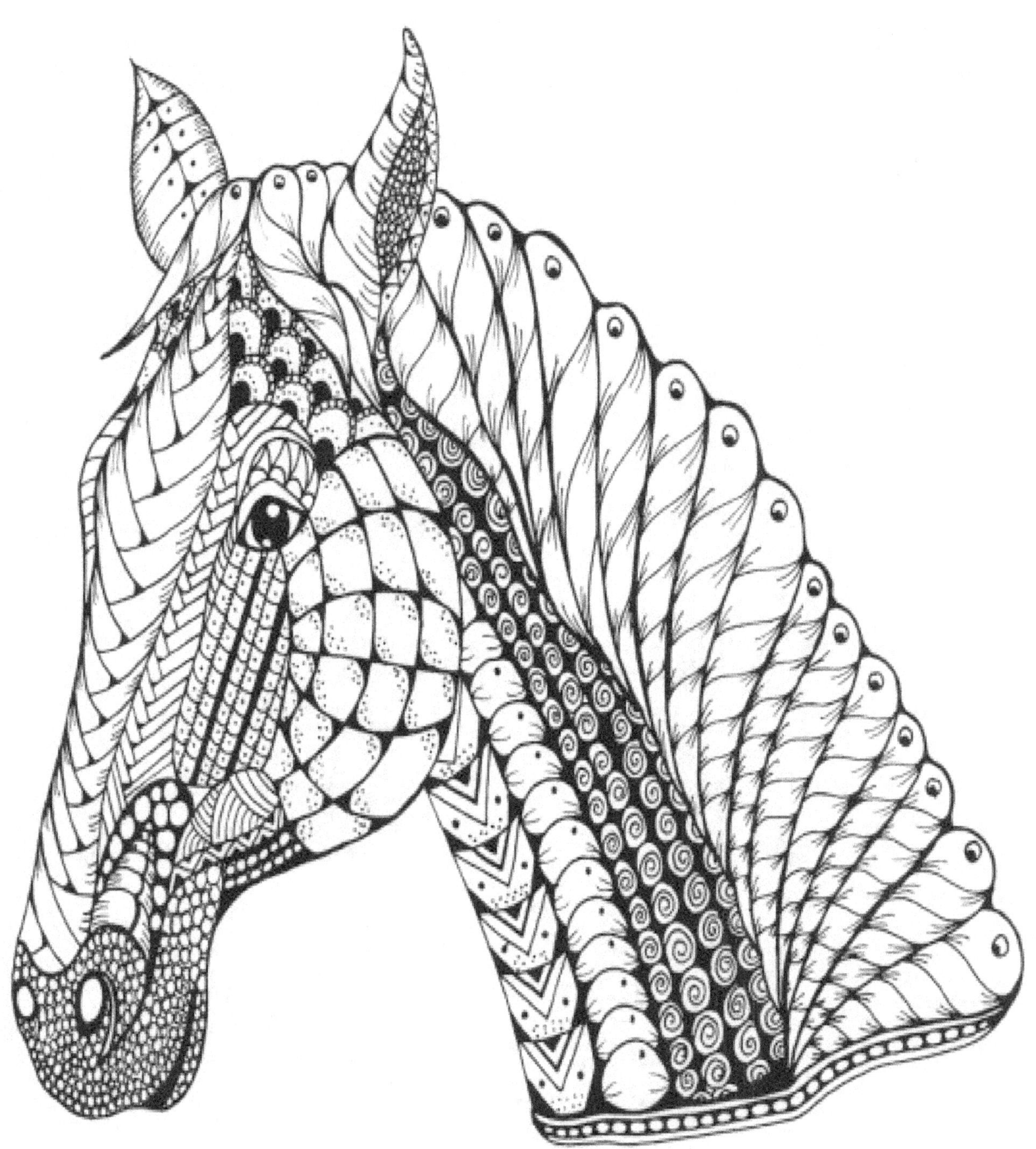

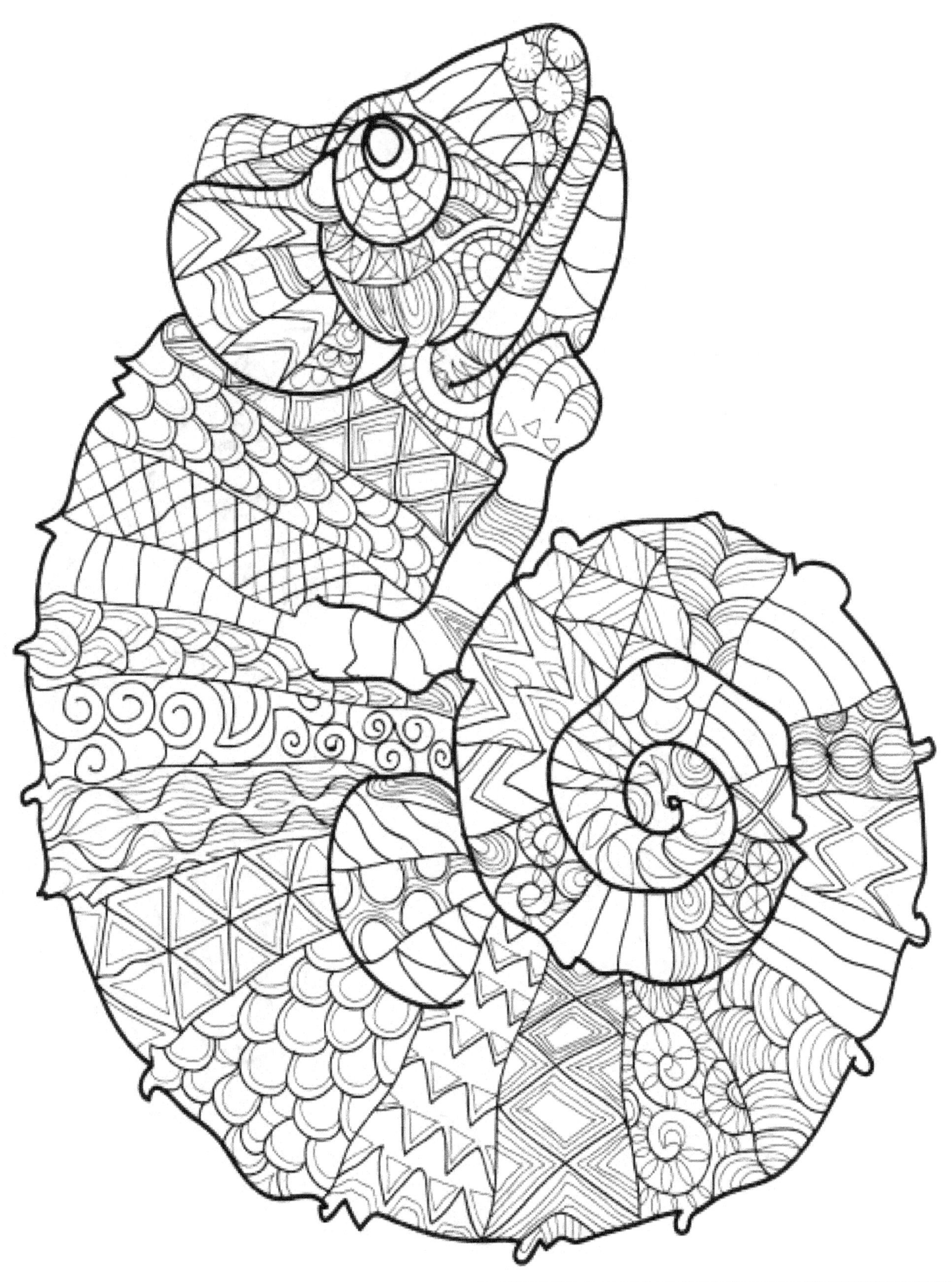

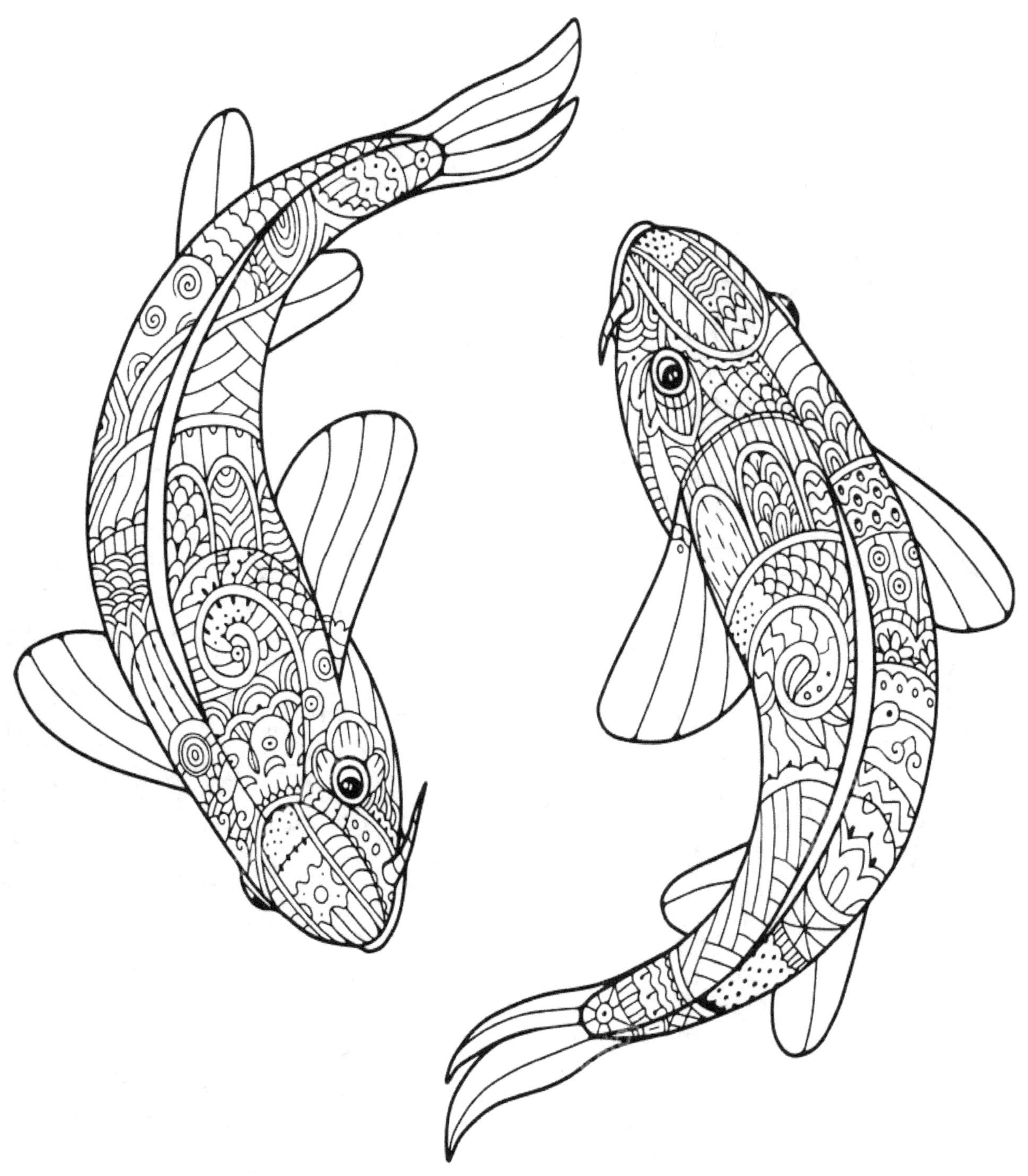

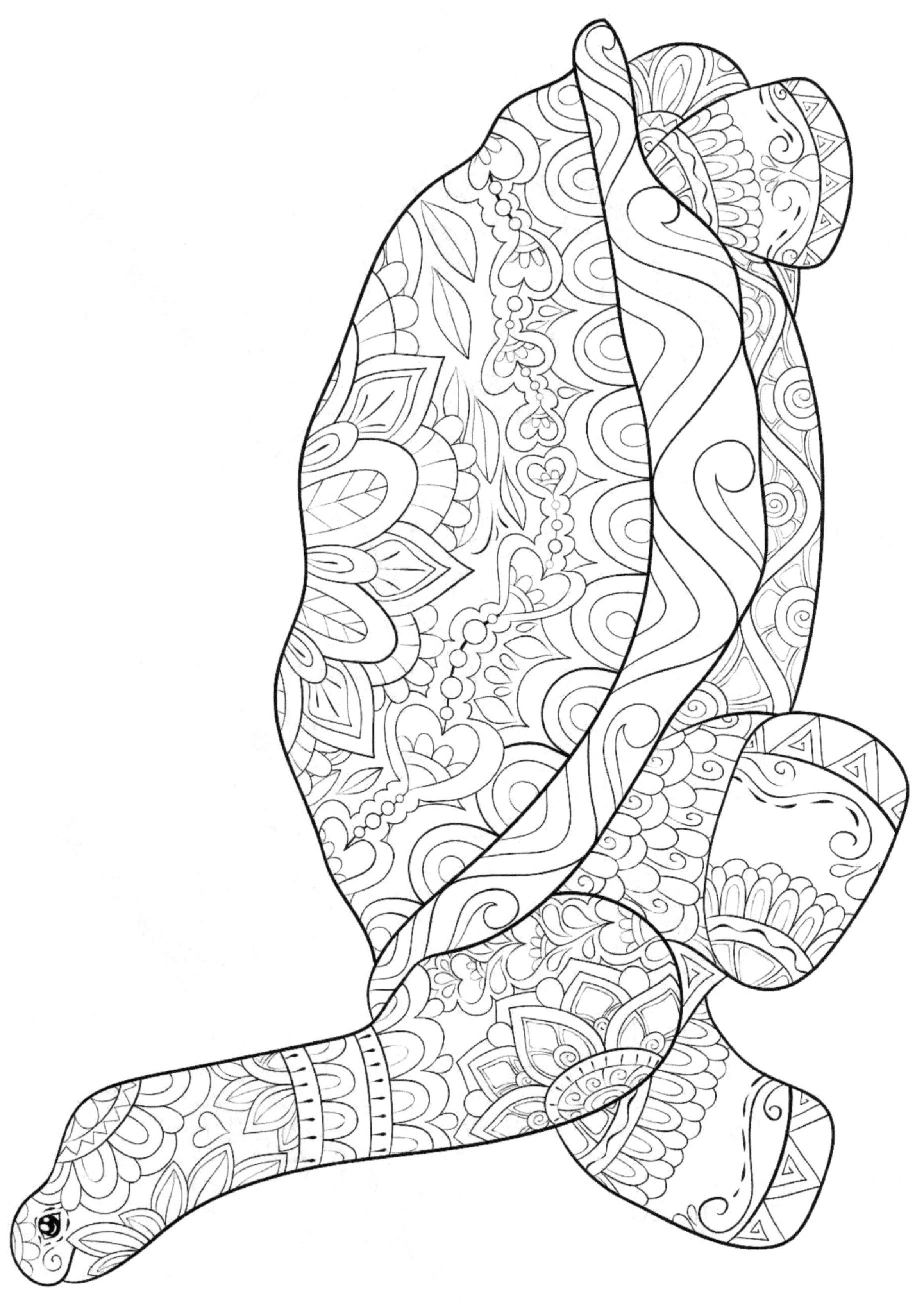

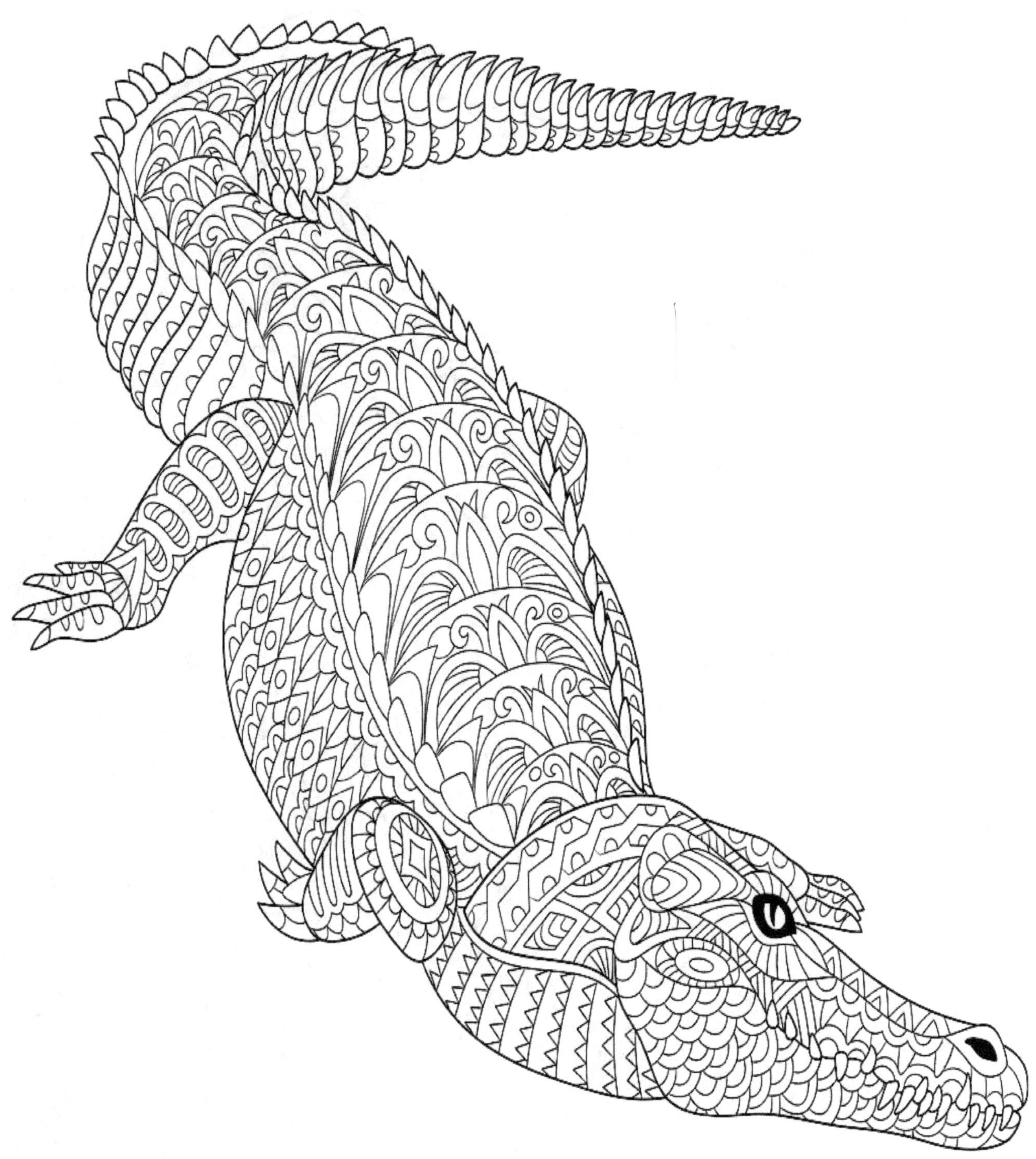